MONKLAND
The Canal That Made Money

by

GUTHRIE HUTTON

The canal was cut to carry coal into Glasgow and numerous mines were scattered all along the route, but by the time this picture was taken, around 1912, much of the coal was going by rail. This tramway ran from Queenslie pit to the main railway line on the other side of the hill and is seen here crossing the canal beside the Garthamlock Nos. 4 and 5 pits, where a barge waits to be loaded.

First Published in the United Kingdom, 1993
By Richard Stenlake, Ochiltree Sawmill, The Lade, Ochiltree, Ayrshire KA18 2NX
Telephone: 02907 266

Iron brought a level of trade to the Monkland that few other canals in Britain could match. But much of it went to build the railways which themselves owed much to the invention of the steam engine by the man who built the canal, James Watt; and the railway eventually killed his canal – iron and irony.

INTRODUCTION

There was a lot of coal under Glasgow in 1769, but the price, controlled by a small group of mine owners, was high and getting higher. A few miles away in the Monklands, coal was cheap and plentiful, but poor roads meant that it stayed there. The city magistrates knew that if they could solve this transport problem, they would break the monopoly. So they asked James Watt to survey for a canal.

He presented two schemes; one to join the Clyde at the Broomielaw would require an expensive flight of locks, while the other, stopping short of the city at Germiston, had no locks and would cost less than half the more ambitious scheme. The magistrates settled for the cheaper option.

Watt began cutting at Sheepford on 26th June 1770. His inexperienced contractors soon encountered difficult ground conditions, but for three years they inched towards Glasgow until the money ran out. The canal had not reached its planned terminal, but Watt, who would have been regarded as a good canal engineer if he hadn't built steam engines too, left the job, confident he had done enough to bring down the price of coal in Glasgow.

He was wrong. More money had to be raised in 1780 to push the canal on to Blackhill and, at a lower level, from Blackhill to Townhead, but even that was not enough. More improvements were carried out between 1790 and 1793. Locks were built at Blackhill to join the upper and lower levels together and the canal was extended, east through locks at Sheepford to the North Calder Water and west to the Forth and Clyde Canal at Port Dundas. The old coal monopoly could at last be broken.

These final improvements were paid for by three brothers, Andrew, John and James Stirling who had become sole owners of the canal in 1789. But their faith was justified; coal was now pouring into Glasgow and the canal was paying dividends. Shares that had traded at £15 in 1781 soared to £1200 in 1815, but the Stirlings' interests in the canal ceased around this time when they got into difficulties with other ventures.

The development of the iron industry in Coatbridge in the 1830s generated so much business that the growth of railways caused barely a blip on the upward graph of profit and even the passenger services continued to thrive. The Forth and Clyde Canal Company bought the Monkland in 1846 for the equivalent of £3400 a share and in 1867 the two canals were bought by the Caledonian Railway, but their fierce rivalry with the North British Railway for the iron business forced trade off the canal on to the railway. In twenty years traffic halved and by the mid 1930's the canal was disused. It was abandoned in 1950. In the 1960s most of the track through Coatbridge was filled in and later the section from Townhead to Easterhouse was buried under the M8 motorway.

The Monkland was never glamorous, but even in its industrial hey-day people enjoyed its amenity value too. Now the bits that have survived at Faskine and Drumpellier are reverting to attractive countryside and there are plans to dredge out some of the infilled sections too. The Monkland Canal is making a qualified comeback.

Guthrie Hutton. August 1993

WOODHALL, CALDERBANK.

The early history of the Monkland Canal is dominated by the supply of two things; money and water. Contrary to popular belief canals are not stagnant, they use huge volumes of water and when Parliament sanctioned a canal, it also approved the building of reservoirs and the diverting of rivers and streams to supply it. But the catchment area approved for the Monkland Canal was much smaller than that for the Forth and Clyde and when that canal sought to take water needed by the Monkland the future looked bleak. An agreement however was reached in 1787 to supply water through the Monkland to the Forth and Clyde; to honour it, the canal was extended to Calderbank and new reservoirs were made.

WOODHALL, CALDERBANK, AIRDRIE.

The great Hillend Reservoir, believed at the time to be the largest in the world, was built at Caldercruix to feed water into the North Calder Water which was then directed into the canal at Calderbank. By the end of the century the canal was drawing water from Johnstone Loch, Bishop Loch, Woodend Loch, Lochend Loch, Black Loch and Hillend and later in the 19th century from Lilly Loch and Roughrigg Reservoir. The channel at Calderbank starts as a narrow, shallow feeder, but this quickly widens out into navigable canal. This cottage beside the feeder was called Canal Basin Cottage (which shows how short the feeder was) and the cottages behind the trees were known as Canal Row.

Iron working had been established in the Calder Gorge late in the eighteenth century and coal mines were opened up too. Quay facilities were provided for this growing industry and a rectangular basin west of Calderbank was linked by railway to pits on the south side of the Calder. Barges on the canal were known as scows – an old Scots word for 'flat bottomed boat'. These were not the narrow boats of English canals, nobody lived on them. They were simple craft that made few concessions to the weather, protected neither cargo nor crew and were loaded, as in this picture, to allow little freeboard. Screw propelled steam scows started to take over from horse drawn boats in the mid 1850s.

Despite the huge number of these nameless scows, the canal is famous for just one boat, the 'Vulcan', the first iron boat to be built in Scotland. She was built at Thomas Wilson's Faskine boatyard to drawings prepared by a civil engineer, William Crighton, under the guidance of John Robison, a member of the council of the Forth and Clyde Canal Company. The blacksmiths John and Thomas Smellie had a tough time bending the angle iron frame from flat bar, to which were riveted the malleable iron plate. Sceptics who had scoffed at the idea of floating iron were confounded when the 61'0" vessel was launched in May 1819 to begin her career as a passage (passenger) boat on the Forth and Clyde Canal. She was scrapped in 1873.

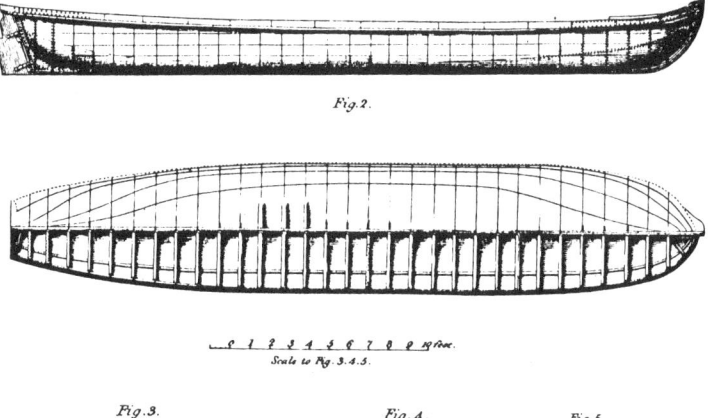

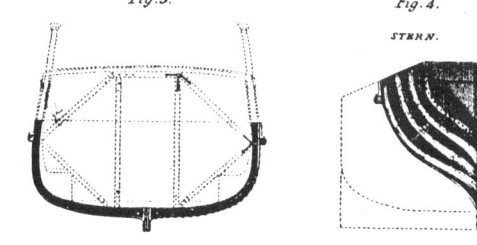

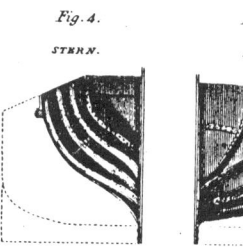

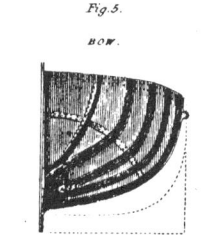

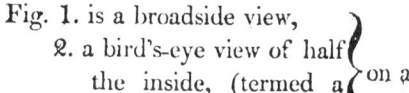

Fig. 1.

MALLEABLE IRON PASSAGE BOAT.

Fig. 2.

Scale to Fig. 3. 4. 5.

Fig. 3. *Fig. 4.* *Fig. 5.*
         STERN.   BOW.

Fig. 1. is a broadside view,
     2. a bird's-eye view of half the inside, (termed a half breadth plan,) } on a small scale.
     3. a midship section,
     4. part of the inside, (looking aft,) -   -   - } on a larger scale.
     5. Do. do. forward,   -
     6. a small part of a rib and plates, (much enlarged.)

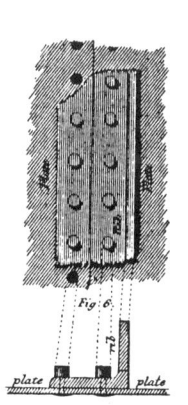

Fig. 6.
plate   plate

The plates were supplied by Calderbank Iron Works which was renowned for high quality plates and no doubt the closeness of the works to the boatyard was a factor in deciding that the 'Vulcan' should be built at Faskine. 'Vulcan' was a significant step forward in the development of shipbuilding in Scotland and many years later the canal was to benefit when the shipyards on the Clyde needed huge quantities of plate shipped to them from the iron works of Coatbridge. In 1986 the Clyde honoured its debt again when Monklands District Council ordered this full size replica from British Shipbuilders Training Ltd.

She was built at Linthouse as a Manpower Services Commission scheme for long term unemployed craftsmen. The materials were new, mild steel was used instead of malleable iron and rolled steel angle iron replaced the Smellie's hand made angle. But the 20th century craftsmen didn't have the furnaces that were available to their predecessors and they had to re-learn old skills, like riveting. She was moved by road from Linthouse to Govan where she entered the water for the first time, for tilt trials. From there, she was taken to the 1988 Glasgow Garden Festival, to be fitted out as part of the District Council's Festival display. She is now at Summerlee Heritage Centre waiting for the canal to be restored between there and Drumpellier.

If 'Vulcan' earned Faskine a place in history, neighbouring Palacecraig's claim to fame is as the southern terminal of the Monkland and Kirkintilloch Railway, the first public railway in Scotland, opened in 1826 (these bridge abutments of the extension over the canal at Palacecraig were photographed in 1960). It was promoted by many of the mine owners and its meandering line provided their collieries with a means of transporting coal to the Forth and Clyde Canal at Kirkintilloch. Although the railway threatened trade on the Monkland Canal to Glasgow, its primary purpose must have been to gain access through the recently completed Union Canal to the lucrative Edinburgh market. There were other early railways in the area too, but the one that directly threatened the canal was the Garnkirk and Glasgow, opened in 1831.

It ran from a junction with the Monkland and Kirkintilloch at Gartsherrie to Glasgow's Townhead but because it stopped short of the deep water of the Forth and Clyde at Port Dundas the Monkland was able to reduce its rates and thereby resist the challenge. The proliferation of railway lines criss-crossing the Monklands reflects the area's pioneering role in the development of the Scottish rail network and earned Coatbridge the nickname 'Crewe of the North'. One of the most impressive features is this viaduct carrying the Caledonian Railway's Airdrie branch line over the canal at Sheepford, seen here in the 1950's looking towards Coatdyke. The bay on the left had to be angled to match the line of the canal as it swung away from Sheepford Locks.

Sheepford Locks were completed in 1792 as part of the extension of the canal to Calderbank. The two locks, separated by a basin, raised the canal 21'0". Photographs of them are rare, but this aerial view from the 1940s gives a good impression of the layout. Locks Street crosses the tail of the top lock and beyond the locks is the railway viaduct seen on the previous page. The weeded up canal below the locks shows that the end was near; the locks were demolished in 1962. Passenger boats operated from below Sheepford Locks. One boat took the passengers to Blackhill where they had to walk down the hill to join another boat to complete their 2½ hour journey to Townhead in Glasgow.

TUBE WORKS OF A. AND J. STEWART.

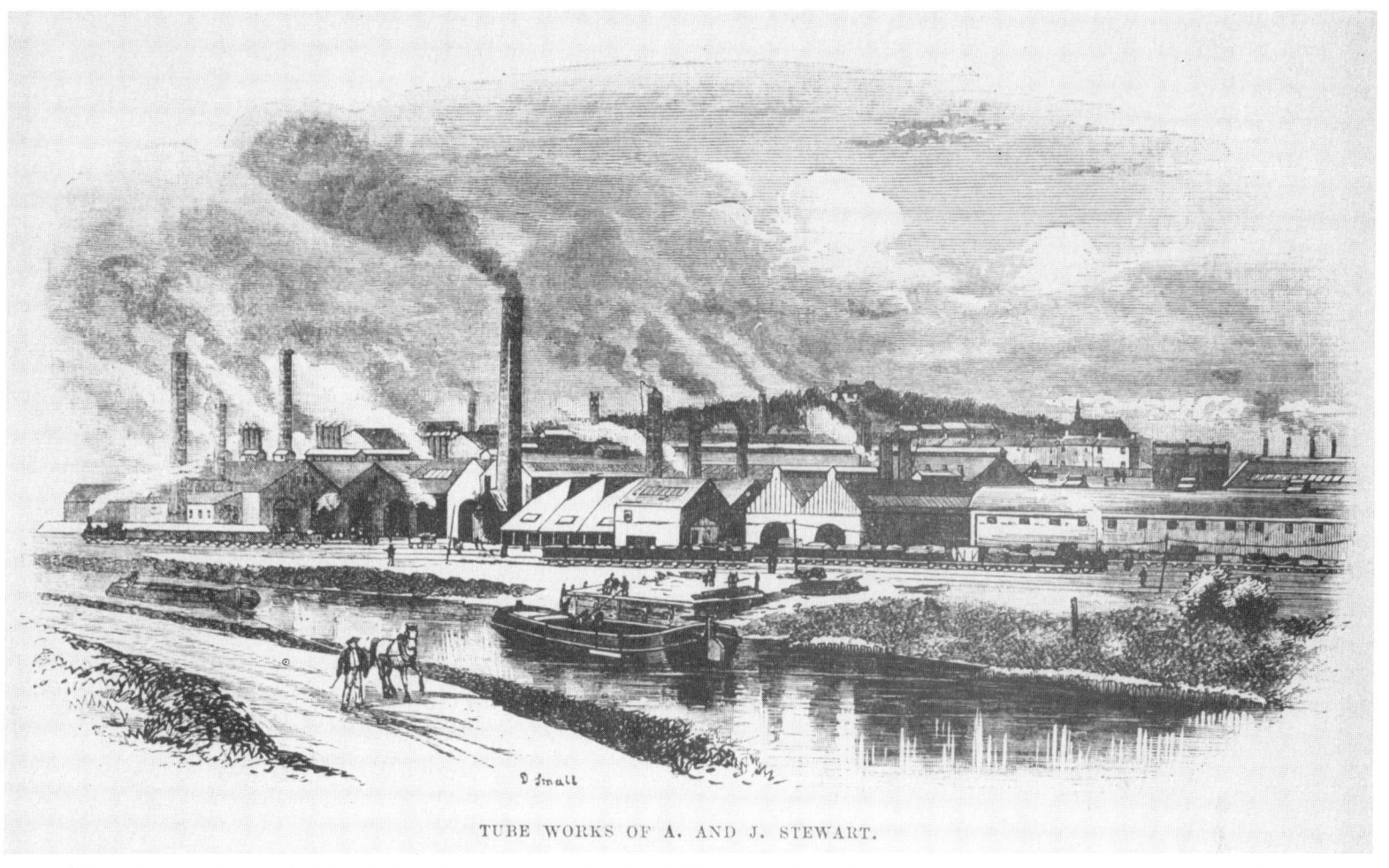

When the iron industry of Coatbridge developed rapidly after 1830 it needed two things, a means of transport and a supply of cooling water. The canal provided both and the banks were quickly lined with iron works of all kinds like A and J Stewart's tube works at Coatdyke. Stewarts later became the iron and steel giant Stewarts and Lloyds. The canal was cut in 110 yard lots and without any formal ceremony the first of Watt's contractors, James Johnstone, began digging here in 1770. But he had struck a bad bargain at 1¾ pence per cubic yard because heavy rain combined with clay soil to make his job difficult. Watt later compensated him by allowing more generous terms on other work.

Coatbridge and its iron works were once described as 'no worse place out of hell'. The actor, who wrote on the back of this postcard of the Clifton Iron Works, clearly agreed and wanted a reminder of the 'awful' experience. An odd memento, perhaps, but the Theatre Royal was just across the street from the works and the blazing furnaces would not have been the kind of bright lights most performers had in mind when they took to the boards. Iron works were sandwiched between the canal and the town's Main Street and in places were built side by side with houses. The smoke, dirt and noise made this 'iron heart' of Coatbridge an unpleasant place to live in, even the canal water is said to have steamed from the number of works using it for cooling.

Excavating wet sand in this deep cutting west of Coatbank Street was a major problem for Watt. The contractors took a year to complete the section and eventually had to build wharf walls and turf banks to contain the unstable ground. The finished canal gave problems too. In 1791 it burst into Coats Pit, drowning six miners. The bridge taking the towpath over the entrance to the Dundyvan Branch Canal can be seen to the left of the prominent fire station tower. Coatbridge Iron Works is to the left of the bridge and East Canal Street runs along the top of the embankment on the right.

THE BRIDGES
COATBRIDGE

There can be few places where so many routes cross the one spot as 'The Bridges', this wonderfully haphazard collection of road, rail and pedestrian bridges over the canal in central Coatbridge. Watt started the process by building an aqueduct over the Gartsherrie Burn (which collapsed and had to be repaired in 1858) and a bridge to take the Airdrie Road over the canal. The slightly arched low bridge leading up from the tow path was built for horses to cross from the main canal to the Gartsherrie Branch. It was known (with stunning originality) as 'Horse Bridge'. The lattice girder railway bridge replaced a dangerous level crossing on the Monkland and Kirkintilloch Railway. The canal quays here were known as Daddy Young's harbour.

Hidden behind Horse Bridge is the entrance to (to give it its full name) the Gartsherrie, Hornock and Summerlee branch of the canal. There were more branch canals on the Monkland than on the whole of the Scottish Canal System put together – and most of them were in Coatbridge (Scotland's Venice perhaps?). Dixon's Cut ran south from Sheepford to William Dixon's Calder Pit and Iron Works. The Dundyvan Branch, also on the south side of the canal just east of 'The Bridges' was originally cut to serve coal mines, but was later extended to the iron works and had extensive railway transhipment basins developed at its terminus. The branch canal network was completed by a side cut to the Langloan Iron Works and the Gartsherrie Branch.

17

On the left of the Gartsherrie Branch in this view of Summerlee Iron works is the Gartsherrie Burn. It was diverted from its original meandering course into culverts so that the branch canal could be cut on its bed. Earlier it had been used as a feeder for the main canal until its modest flow was supplanted by Hillend Reservoir. The Gartsherrie Branch was originally planned to serve coal mines and was still unfinished in 1830 when the Baird brothers set up their Gartsherrie Iron Works at its terminus (seen on the opposite page with the canal dwarfed by the great blast furnaces). It was the start of the iron industry that was to transform both Coatbridge and the Monkland Canal.

The rapid expansion of the industry was due first to David Mushet's discovery of blackband ironstone near Coatdyke, then to the invention of the hot blast process of iron smelting by James Beaumont Neilson and finally to the flouting of his patent by the Bairds. The number of blast furnaces and puddling furnaces increased rapidly and their voracious appetite for both iron ore and coal had a phenomenal effect on the canal. The 50,000 tons of coal carried in 1793 had steadily increased to over 100,000 tons by 1830, but in 1831 the amount of coal carried leaped to over 200,000 tons. By 1850 the combined total of coal and iron had topped the million and in 1863 it reached its peak of one and a half million tons.

The infant railways were still seen as feeder systems to the canal which at that time was the only transport system capable of handling the huge volume of raw materials in, finished product out, generated by this unfettered development. The main blast furnace plants, Gartsherrie, Dundyvan and Calder were set up on existing branch canals. So too was Summerlee Iron Works which began operations in 1836 beside the Gartsherrie Branch. The works, seen here on the bend of the branch canal, closed down in 1930. The site is now occupied by the Summerlee Heritage Trust who have excavated the bases of the great blast furnaces and restored Howes Basin, in the foreground, as exhibits.

The Bairds developed much of urban Coatbridge with their wealth from iron and coal and as if to crown their town planning ventures they provided most of the funds to build Gartsherrie Church at the top of Baird Street. Here the church overlooks this scene of bare bottomed weans swimming in the Gartsherrie Branch opposite Summerlee Iron Works. Not quite the image of danger, disease and industrial filth the canal's detractors put about in the 1950s. The bridge carrying the towpath over the entrance to Howes Basin can be seen in the background. It was a coal transhipment basin originally associated with the Monkland and Kirkintilloch Railway.

There are great contradictions in Scotland; we marvel at the heroic failure of the Caledonian Canal and hold the Forth and Clyde in nostalgic affection, but have gone to extraordinary lengths to obliterate the country's one really successful canal from the face of the map. From Sikeside through the centre of Coatbridge to Blairhill the canal has been filled in and the towpath dug up and replaced by … a path without a canal beside it. And they gave somebody an award for doing that! The picture, looking west, shows the infilling at the point where the Gartsherrie Branch joined the main line between 'The Bridges'.

Even the Government connived by giving 90% grants towards the cost. Hundreds of thousands of pounds were spent in the 1960s to achieve effectively nothing and it still costs money to maintain and insure because, hidden from view, the water flows through these pipes (seen here heading west under Merrystone Bridge) to feed the Forth and Clyde Canal. If the money had been spent on dredging, landscaping and upgrading the canal and its branches, it would have created an unrivalled asset for Coatbridge. The flow also had to be maintained to supply cooling water to the Gartcosh Steel Works, which in its day was a nice little earner for the canal's owners, British Waterways.

Merrystone (or Maryston) Bridge was built later than other bridges and incorporates refinements like stonework abutments with integrated bases for gas lighting standards and decorative cast iron railings. It is also much broader than other bridges, perhaps because it gives access to the more affluent middle class housing of Blairhill. The picture taken in 1924 looks across the bridge to the west with a couple of scows moored on the other side. The bridge still spans the pedestrian walkway that replaced the tow path.

The delights of pleasure boating, a feature on other canals in the late 19th and early 20th centuries were also enjoyed on the Monkland. Coal barges were scrubbed clean for special trips which, as this picture of a wonderfully overcrowded steam scow shows, were very popular. This boat, known as the Summerlee 'Jenny', is seen here on a works outing at Blairhill. The building on the left is now Nos. 42 and 43 King Street, the road running up the hill to the left is Torrisdale Street and the buildings at the top are on the corner with Albany Street. The trippers would have sailed out to Drumpellier or beyond to Easterhouse or Provan Hall for a picnic on the fields. Sunday School trips were popular elsewhere on the canal too.

King Street and Canal, Coatbridge

Looking east in 1904 from Blair Bridge to the newly built 'up-market' houses of King Street. Here people could live in comparative cleanliness to the west and therefore up-wind for most of the year, of all the smoke and dirt of the iron works. West End Park, originally called Yeomanry Park, was beside the towpath here. The eastern boundary of the park was formed by the Langloan Branch canal which was cut to serve the Langloan Iron Works, founded in 1841. An 80 yard tunnel took the branch canal under Bank Street and Buchanan Street to terminate in a wide basin beside the iron works.

Blair Bridge,   Coatbridge.

The timber deck and stone abutments of Blair Bridge are typical of the Monkland bridges. In front of it the narrowed channel (also in the picture on the previous page) was used to dam the canal. Stop planks were slid down slots in the stonework to allow the canal to be drained for cleaning or closed in the event of a breach. Watt considered an alternative route for the canal west of 'The Bridges' which would have taken it closer to the Luggie Burn, but he opted for this route round Blairhill instead. A coal pit on the other side of the bridge was sandwiched between the canal and the cottages on the right. The next mile and a half of canal beside Drumpellier Park is still in water and a slipway has been built.

ON THE CANAL, NEAR COATBRIDGE.

The Drumpellier Home Farm Bridge was built at the turn of the century on abutments set back from the canal maintaining the channel width. When the canal was closed it was also blocked by a drowned culvert here. Now a replica of the bridge has been built, the culvert removed and the canal dredged to restore this scene to what it was. Judging by the number of pictures of it, the Home Farm bridge was a focus for local photographers, one of whom managed to prove that punting is not just an idiosyncratic English pastime. Watt had difficulties here with swelling peat moss which required repeated excavation. Further west another short branch canal was cut to a coal mine.

Garnheath Bridge, the original Drumpellier Estate Bridge, is seen in the top picture with Garnheath Cottage beside it. The bridge was superseded by the Home Farm bridge and the ruined offside abutment would indicate a need to replace it sometime before 1904 when the picture postcard was used. The lower picture, co-incidentally taken in 1904, shows the same ruined abutment, but a peculiar and apparently private footbridge' (known by those who remember it as the 'shooglie bridge') now spans the canal. Left of the small arch are indications of an arched construction to form the main span. Watt's original bridges are believed to have been stone arches, but none survived into the era of photographs as evidence. Bridges on this canal are usually referred to by name and it is rare to see one given a number.

Between the present A752 and M73 roads was the Cuilhill Gullet, a transhipment terminal for the Drumpellier Railway. The railway was built in 1847 (and extended in 1854) to transport coal from a number of pits to the canal and by 1849 was sending 900 boat loads of coal a year to Glasgow. It was a remarkable development at a time of great railway expansion, but it continued in operation until 1896. The canal was on an embankment and the railway had to cross to the north side creating an island of railway tracks and loading wharves between the existing canal and a new channel which was cut to the north of the terminal. The unusual concave wharf walls had distinctive iron hooks in them, some are still attached to the ruins today. There was a small boatyard at Cuilhill too.

It is possible to follow the overgrown line of the filled in canal from Drumpellier to Cuilhill and west for another mile. Netherhouse Bridge still spans the dry channel and as if to prove that some things never change people still come from distant places to dump rubbish there. The imposing steeple of Bargeddie Parish Church dominates the countryside here. It can be seen for miles and will have been a conspicuous landmark for the canal men. Some of their early boats could let down a Dutch keel and, in a fair wind, hoist a sail in open country. No doubt the horses approved of this labour saving arrangement!

The visible remains of the canal disappear at where the old mining village of West Maryston, known (affectionately) as 'The Hole', used to be. From there a road roughly follows the line of the canal to Easterhouse which was once a small mining village lying mainly to the south of the canal.

Between Easterhouse and Townhead the canal has been destroyed and replaced by six lanes of motorway. But the route remains, every bend and sweep has been perfectly preserved in tarmac and, as at Easterhouse many of the bridges, both vehicular and pedestrian, are built in the same locations and share the same names as their canal predecessors. (see illustration 1 inside back cover).

Easterhouse school, seen here just left of centre, was on the north side of the canal. The foreground shed belonged to a Mr McSporran whose stables there ensured that boats were often moored alongside, 'though the scow in the foreground is believed to be one used for Sunday School outings. When parents asked their children where they had been playing, they got the answer 'nae place', but 'nae place' was up behind McSporran's stable and the truth that they had been near the canal would have earned a skelping. There were numerous pits in the area and mining was the principal industry for villages like Easterhouse, West Maryston, Swinton and Baillieston.

Bartiebeith farm can be seen tucked in behind the large tree on the right of this tranquil country scene. Just beyond the bend was Hallhill transhipment basin which was associated with a mineral railway from Springhill Colliery. Modern Easterhouse has now been built on the parkland either side of the canal here.

At Bartiebeith the motorway occupies the same shallow cutting that the canal did. It's as if the 20th century simply updated the old transport system without, sadly, giving proper regard to what was being destroyed in the process. Initially it was called the Monkland Motorway, but the signs now just say 'M8'. (see illustration 2 inside back cover).

Bartiebeith Bridge was known locally as the 'Ruffian' or 'Bully Ruffian' bridge which was Glasgow slang for Bellerophon a name it acquired after Napoleon Bonaparte had surrendered to the Captain of HMS Bellerophon in 1815. The picture, looking east, shows a scow and a steam scow alongside the loading piers of the Provan Hall Colliery and Fireclay Works, with the 'Ruffian Bridge' in the background. A large modern furniture warehouse now occupies the ground to the left of where the boats are moored.

The title of this picture presumably refers to 'greater Shettleston', because the photograph taken from Milncroft Bridge is looking toward the Cranhill Fireclay Works which later became piggeries. The cottage must have doubled as a local shop, because the writer describes it to his son as; 'cottage by the canal and Teddy, but you can't see Teddy because he has gone inside to buy chocolates' signed 'Dad'.

Through the 1950s and early 60s public hostility to the derelict canal grew and an equally hostile press responded to drowning tragedies by calling it the 'killer canal'. When the motorway plans were announced opinion was so heavily weighted against the canal that even canal enthusiasts, south of the border, thought it would be "...just as well to give the poor old canal a decent burial." And boy, was it buried! (See illustrations 3a and 3b inside back cover).

This view of a horse drawn scow west of Milncroft Bridge is unusual because scows going west were normally fully loaded. But the picture was taken around 1910 and the empty scow is perhaps a sign of declining trade. The horse is beside the foot of some prominent bings of chemical waste which were known to generations of Glasgow youngsters as the 'sugarallie mountains', because they looked like confectionery. Three blocks of high flats now dominate the scene. All these old photographs between Glasgow and Drumpellier were taken looking east. This may be co-incidence, or it may be because people wanted to turn their backs on the encroaching grimy city, or it may simply be that they were all taken on Sunday afternoon walks, with the sun in the west.

These chimneys belonged to the Gartcraig Fireclay Works which was just to the west of Jessie's Bridge, beside the village of Ruchazie. There were a number of fireclay works associated with coal mines east of Glasgow; Gartcraig was linked by tramway to the Gartcraig Colliery. Just visible above the hillside on the left are the chimney tops of houses in Gartcraig Rows.

The advantages of a motorway cutting straight through the outer suburbs to the city centre leaves people who care about canals in a quandary, because the 18th century men of vision who built the canal would probably be delighted that the route they carved out was still of benefit to the city. They might even applaud the foresight of those who updated their canal. (See illustration 4 inside back cover).

The lone house in the centre of this picture is all that was left of Barlinnie Fireclay Works after it was demolished around the turn of the century. The site has apparently been returned to agriculture. Farmland benefitted from Glasgow's principal export – manure (both animal and human), until of course the city swallowed up this countryside in its inexorable urban spread eastwards. The picture was taken from Smithycroft Bridge, the stone wall on the left is part of the bridge parapet and the road in the foreground is Cumbernauld Road. The chimneys of Gartcraig can be seen on the left.

Barlinnie Prison and Canal

This picture of Barlinnie Prison was taken from Smithycroft Bridge looking east. A postcard of a prison is unusual. Imagine receiving one; you look at the bleak view of austere and unlovely buildings then turn it over to read that universal message; 'Having a lovely time, wish you were here'. The shock could ruin your breakfast as well as a friendship.

But the water supply that dictated so much of the Monkland's history had a final part to play and, as at Coatbridge, extensive and expensive piping was required to ensure that the flow was maintained beneath the motorway. In a corner of Port Dundas a stream, that last saw daylight at Drumpellier, still pours millions of gallons, daily into the basins of the Forth and Clyde Canal. (See illustration 5 inside back cover).

The photographer here has somehow managed to miss Smithycroft Bridge, just out of view on the right of this atmospheric picture. All of these buildings have now gone, but just to make sure that some aspect of our heritage has been preserved, the Lethamhill Golf Course, on the hill behind the tenement block has been left intact! Riddrie youngsters would stock up at an apparently wonderful ice cream shop in the red sandstone tenement and walk out along the tow path into the country. Always to the east, because to the west were the (dangerous) Blackhill Locks and they were 'out of bounds'.

CANAL LOCKS, RIDDRIE.

The terminal reached by Watt in 1773 was near Barlinnie and connected to Glasgow by a cart road. Ten years later the canal had been extended to Blackhill and another cut made from the base of the hill to Townhead. For a further ten years coal was unloaded into wagons at the top and lowered $1/4$ mile on rails down the hill to another barge. This was a cumbersome arrangement and it was clear that the only way the canal would achieve its potential was if locks were built, but with no money to pay for them and hopelessly inadequate water supplies to feed them, the canal looked doomed. Most of the proprietors cut their losses, leaving the Stirling brothers as sole owners of the canal. They set about extending the canal, developing the water supplies and building locks at Blackhill.

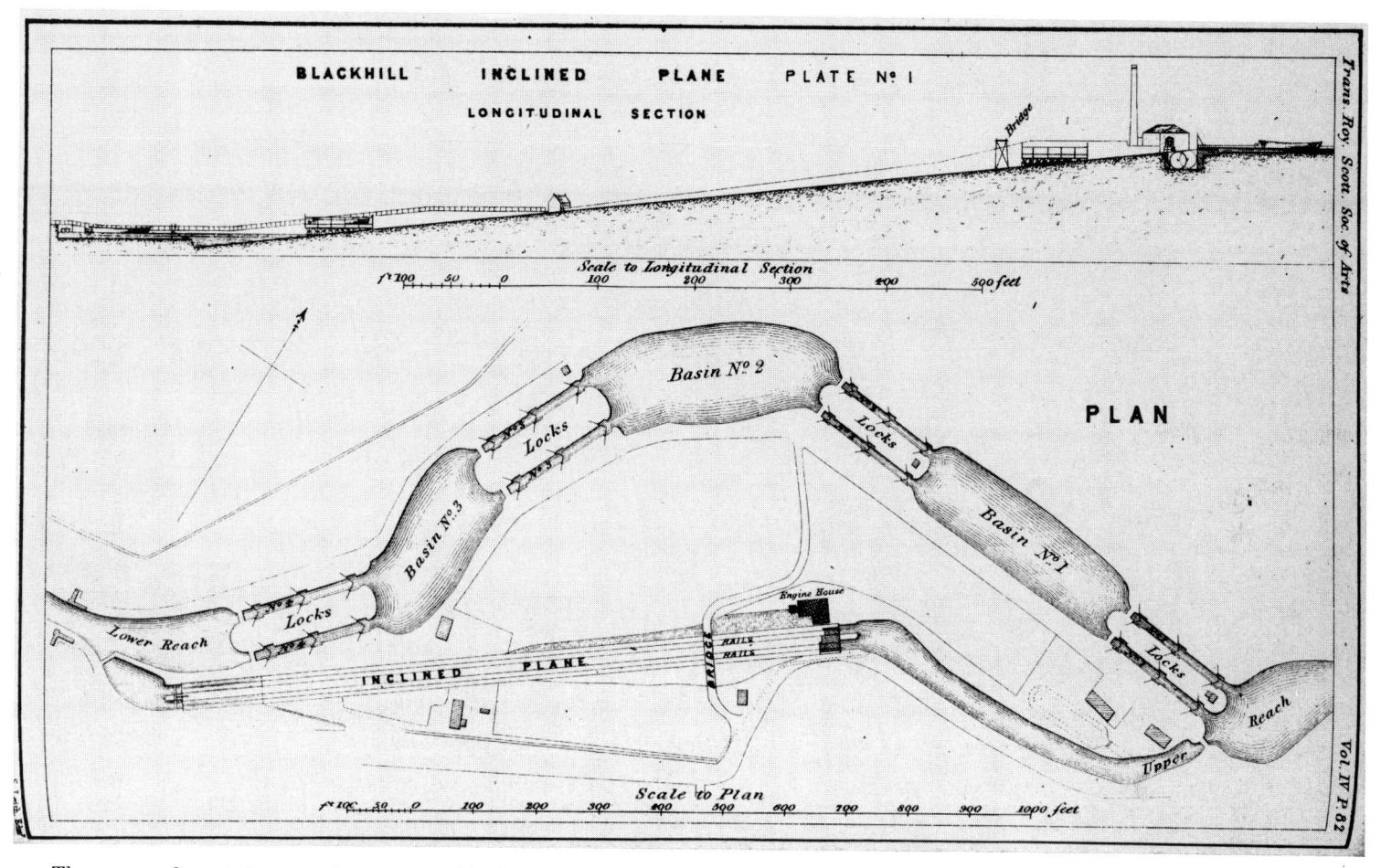

There were four staircase pairs separated by basins, each lock had a fall of 12′0″, each pair, 24′0″ and the whole flight, 96′0″. They were completed in 1793, but by the early 1830s so many boats wanted to use them they had become a bottleneck. One solution to the problem was to construct an inclined plane, a system where boats would be floated into iron caissons and run up and down the hill on rails, by-passing the locks. The idea was not adopted and new locks, creating a double set of staircase pairs were completed in 1841. But trade continued to increase and this, combined with the old problem of water supply (lack of water stopped the canal for six weeks in 1849), meant that the inclined plane was an idea whose time had come.

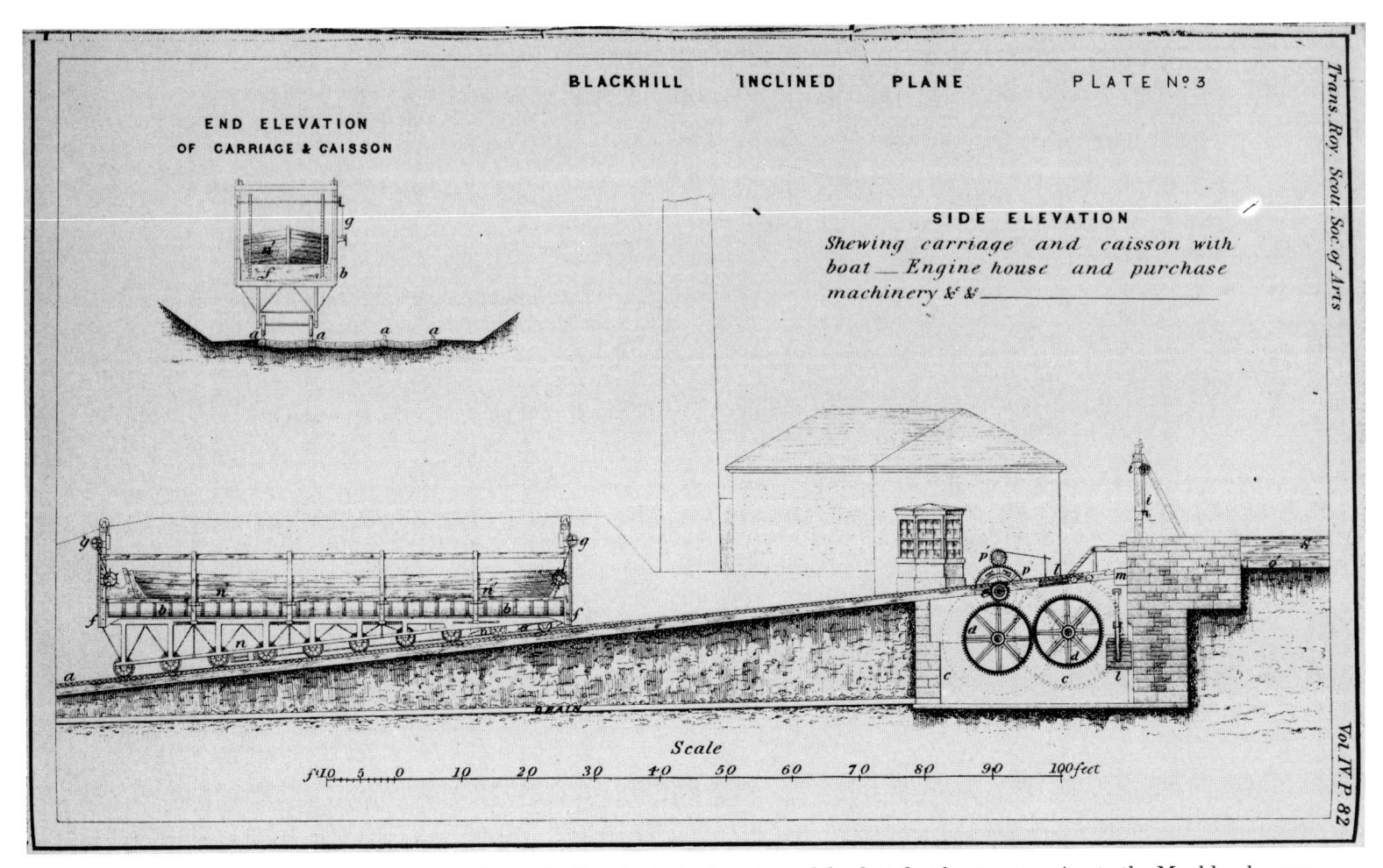

It was built in 1850 by Glasgow engineer James Leslie who took advantage of the fact that boats returning to the Monklands were usually empty. He could therefore reduce the load on the axles of the caissons by only providing for the unloaded boats to go uphill on the incline, while loaded boats went down the locks. The caissons were only 2'9" deep to minimise the amount of water in them and they had wash boards to prevent spillage. They were shaped to cradle the boats and carry them partially aground. The plane was only used during the six or seven months when water supplies were low, even so an average of 7,500 boats a year used the incline in the 1850s. The huge volume of traffic meant that the boilers of the engine house could be kept in steam all the time with no energy lost waiting for the next boat.

Blackhill Locks, Riddrie

The plane worked until 1887 when the drop in traffic meant that it was no longer economical to keep the boilers fired up for the occasional boat. It fell into disuse and was scrapped. It was the only canal incline built in Scotland, yet as with so many of Scotland's great engineering achievements it established many of the principals that are still being used on inclines in other parts of the world. It also ensure that writers of canal history books would, for ever more, have to mention the Monkland Canal. But Glasgow folk simply called it the 'Gazoon'. Believed to be a Glaswegianisation of the word 'cassion', it somehow seems to sum up the almost casual way that the people of this great city accept greatness all around them as if it were the most natural thing in the world. Which, of course, it is!

The locks were still in a reasonable condition in the 1950s when this picture of the south top lock was taken. The height of the gate clearly shows the 5′ 0″ operating depth of the canal and the water pouring over the cill emphasises the cavernous depth of the chamber. The towpath ran between the locks and inclined plane and bridges were required to take it over the entrances to the plane. The upper bridge can be seen behind the lock here (and can just be seen above the locks in the picture on page 42). It presumably remained intact into the 1950s because there was a boatyard and graving dock on the canal arm leading to the inclined plane. The boatyard was moved from the foot of the locks when they were duplicated in the 1840s.

This picture, also from the 1950s, clearly shows the paired staircase locks at the foot of the flight, with the basin extended between them. The line of where the 'Gazoon' was can be seen on the right, (and on page 45) running down the hill between the Blackhill Cottages. All trace of this line has now been landscaped out of existence and the recent demolition of Riddrie School at the top of the hill has removed the last remaining landmark from this remarkable complex. But people still remember it and, with it, an equally remarkable contradiction to the old Glasgow opposition to canals. Boys (now men in their sixties) would be told by their parents not to go near the canal, but boys will be boys and while they were there other adults would offer them money to dive over the locks into the basins below. A dangerous, but exhilarating and apparently profitable sport.

At the foot of the locks was Provan Gas Works and beside them the Blochairn Steel Works. Despite the impact of this industry one writer in the 1930s described "...the surprising beauty of the northern bank ... with fine hawthorn trees and masses of whin in bloom". He went on "... a photograph taken here might well be shown as a choice piece of quiet river scenery." Sadly, he didn't take one! Fortunately someone, early this century, did take this, possibly the finest picture of the way of life on the canals of Central Scotland. It shows a Gartsherrie coal scow at the wharf east of the Castle Street basin with the tenements of Garngad Hill and Earlston Avenue in the background. The horse is being led by a Mr. Rogan, his family are crewing the boat.

The gallows, where Glasgow hung its wrongdoers, had to be moved from their site above Castle Street to the Castle yard so that the canal could be terminated at this basin in 1783. The basin remained in use after the extension to Port Dundas was completed. As part of that extension a stone bridge was built to carry the towpath over the basin entrance. It was replaced in 1858, but later removed. This picture shows the basin still in use in the 1950s, though by this time only a few desultory piles of coal remain and the coping stones have started to collapse into the cut. When the Carlton cinema was built at the end of the basin, a monument, erected there in 1818 by the Canal Company to three martyred Covenanters, was moved and incorporated into the cinema walls.

The extension to Port Dundas went through a sharp S bend. The motorway took a much gentler line leaving the Castle Street bridge as the only surviving remnant of the canal in the city. It serves little useful function as a pedestrian underpass, but complete with cast iron rubbing strakes still scarred with grooves cut by wet ropes, its value as an ancient monument is inestimable. A branch canal continued north from the outside of the bend before the bridge. It crossed under Garngad (now Royston) Road, turned through 90° and ran mid-way between Garngad Road and Charles Street. It was only wide enough for a single barge and so there were a number of loading bays to serve a warren of iron works, pipe works, mills and foundries. For a time a short extension also crossed under Charles Street.

The Monkland Canal ended at Castle Street Bridge and between there and Port Dundas was a canal that was neither Forth and Clyde nor Monkland. It was known as the 'Cut of Junction'. Initially it was cut to the same dimensions as the Monkland, but was deepened in 1842 and had Forth and Clyde style opening bridges installed at Glebe Street and Port Dundas. This encouraged the great Tennant's Chemical Works to bring their trade up the canal to St. Rollox, in preference to using the Clyde. The canal outside their works was also known as St. Rollox basin and this picture of the infilling operation in the 1960s shows it with Castle Street Bridge at the end and the empty site of Tennant's works beside it.

SELECT BIBLIOGRAPHY

Jean Lindsay	The Canals of Scotland, pub: David and Charles, 1968
E.A. Pratt	Scottish Canals and Waterways, pub: Selwyn and Blount 1922
George Thomson	The Monkland Canal – A Sketch of the Early History, pub; Monklands Library Services Department
Peter Drummond and James Smith	Coatbridge – Three Centuries of Change, pub; Monklands Library Services Department 2nd (rev) edition 1984.
Robert Duncan	Calderbank – An Industrial and Social History, pub; Monklands District Library Services Department
Waterways World	three articles; 'Scottish Revival' by P.J.G. Ransom, August 1986; Vulcan Reforged by P.J.G. Ransom, June 1988 and 'Doon the Gazoon' by David Page, May 1989.
James Cowan	From Glasgow's Treasure Chest, pub; Craig Wilson, 1951
Alan Peden	The Monklands – An Illustrated Architectural Guide, pub; Royal Incorporation of British Architects, 1992.
Don Martin	The Monkland and Kirkintilloch Railway, pub; Strathkelvin District Libraries and Museums, 1976.
Don Martin	The Garnkirk and Glasgow Railway, pub; Strathkelvin District Libraries and Museums, 1981.
Stewart Jackson	My Ain Folk – History of Baillieston and District, pub; Baillieston Community Council.

ACKNOWLEDGEMENTS

It may seem odd to start by acknowledging the help of people long dead, but the fabulous Ordnance Survey maps drawn by the soldiers of Queen Victoria's Army made it possible to visualise what this canal looked like and to identify the locations of many early photographs.

I am grateful to Steve Kay and David Peace of Summerlee Heritage Trust for their help and for the use of photographs on pages 8, 9, 12, 15, 20, 21, 25, 35, 48 and the back cover. I must also thank Willie Miller, Chief Planning Officer with Monklands District Council for the pictures on pages 22 and 23 and for some valuable assistance with research. Thanks too to John Fox and Andy Edgar of Monklands District Libraries for permission to use pictures on pages 11 and 19, to Don Martin of Strathkelvin District Libraries for the pictures on pages 10, 38, 39 and 41, and to M.G.C.W. (Michael) Wheeler one of Scotland's earliest canal enthusiasts who supplied the pictures on pages 46 and 47. The pictures on the title page and page 37 were first published in 'Shettleston Past and Present' and I am grateful to Thomas Waugh for permission to reproduce them. I am grateful to Strathclyde Regional Archives for permission to publish the pictures on pages 45, 49 and 51 and to the Mitchell Library for endlessly dragging those old maps out for me and for permission to use the illustrations on pages 43 and 44. I must also thank the staff at the Baillieston Library for their assistance and use of the picture on page 31, Stuart Marshall for the cover picture and Bob McCutcheon for the drawing on page 7.

And thanks too to John White, whose local contacts were the source for a number of pictures, Nancy Lawton, Johnny Caulfield and many others for their invaluable local knowledge.